MULTIPLE

WAYS

TO

DEFEAT

CORONA

HOW I DID??

MR.N.S.RATHORE

TEACHER BY PROFESSION

email.nrathore1976@gmail.com

<u>DISCLAIMER</u>

- The book Does Not Provide Medical Advice

- The contents of the Site ,such as text ,graphics, images, and other materials created by book or obtained from book' s licensors, and other materials contained on the book (collectively, "Content") are for informational purposes only. The Content is not intended to be a substitute for professional medical advice, diagnosis, or treatment. Always seek the advice of your physician or other qualified health provider with any questions you may have regarding an medical condition. Never disregard professional medical advice or delay in seeking it because of something you have read on the book .

- If you think you may have a medical emergency, call your doctor or emergency immediately. book does not recommend or endorse any specific tests, physicians, products, procedures, opinions, or other information that may be mentioned in the book. Reliance on any information provided by book. appearing on the Site at the invitation as reader ,or other visitors is solely at your own risk.

INDEX

<u>**MY OWN STORY HOW DO I FACE THIS VIRUS CORONA**</u>

My own untold story of covid in year 2020 I got infected with covid-19. in month of June when in whole country india facing lock down . and every body afraid of corona and quarantine.

'how I easily recovered without any kind of assistance of oxygen or any other medicine only because of my good habits .

as I am trained in yoga and I have good habit of 5 to 6 kilometer morning walk and 10 to 15 minutes deep breathing exercises .

In the morning I used to drink two glass luke warm water this helped me a lot during the situation of infection.

I was quite sure that I will not infected at all, but this virus very much infective and effective .

i casually taken the small symptoms. I don't take care when symptoms increase in your body automatically respond for the day's I feel shortfall of oxygen in body. Because of this infection I am unable to have a good sleep.

Everything is fine but some conjunction in throat later on I feel difficult to have breath in that situation. when I am not getting sleep then I utilize that time for the breath over night I put my bed on the top floor/terrace in the open air .

And I start to take deep breath because I feel uneasy so I could not sleep.

so I try to utilize time and start to take the breathing exercise moving around here and there .

Deep meditation ANULOM VILOM from left nostril inhale air and from right nostril Exhale this practice I continued for 2-3 hours later on I feel some drowsiness and I got sleep at night.

for next day I had repeated the same practice again I sleep in open air and have a deep breath and all that exercises. one of the positive aspect about environment is that air purified and quality of air is good because of lockdown.

There is no pollution so after 2 days I feel myself relaxed and feel normalize in situation. I feel easy as now there is no infection in throat I think the healing work done by my body.

even I am not panic about the situation because the situation outside in the hospital is very bad and painfull no one is taking care of you in that situation when there is no medicine and if you go through that trauma then only you can feel pain.

I do not want me to put myself in trouble I keep it secret with me only and isolate myself and I try to do my best throughout the day I used to drink hot water .

Some vaporization to relax my nostril and it gives relax to my chest and clear the breathing route and lubricant with sesame oil.

it also helped me a lot. The most important think which helped me a lot is is the state of mind because my mind remain positive about this situation and it works a lot if your mind have negative attitude then itself creates viruses that is power of mind .

If you are positive state of mind it creates antibodies to fight with all kind of viruses and bacteria in our body. it's our duty and responsibility to stand with mind and give a strength to mind to work positively many people who got infected and faced worsed situation because of that they panic themselves a lot .

which create a pressure on mind and under the pressure mind is not working properly and the virus able to capture such body .But there is a great saying that there is a will there is a way.

so keep yourself positive and keep some good habits .There is many people who are still in such a dilemma and in fear can remove that fear and dilemma because still there is up to 80% of infected need not to hospitalized with their willpower of mind and positive attitude they can easily recovered at their home .

so it's all about my story. it's my own experience I am sharing with you and I feel my myself more confident to face such situation in future also and I am damn sure that my good habits and my positive attitude will definitely come out with flying colours come out with long life living colours.

I wish all my readers healthy and wealthy life because if you keep yourself positive then there is a no one which can defeat you ad your mind as it has immense power to deal all kind of situations I hope you will decide to stand positive side along with your mind..

2. SYMPTOMS OF CORONA

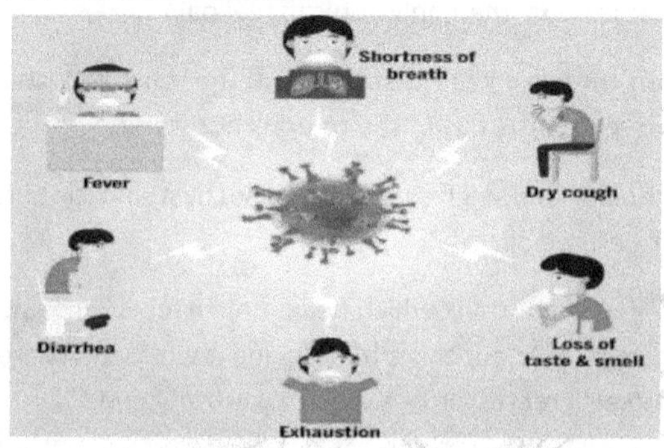

MOST COMMON SYMPTOMS:

FEVER:- if you have fever continous and more than two three days then go for medication
DRY COUGH:- in this situation patient have cough without bulgum or dry cough.
TIREDNESS:- without any heavy work a person feel tired and drowsiness this could be symptoms of corona

LESS COMMON SYMPTOMS:

SORE THROAT:-when you feel your throat choked or conjuction in throat or sore throat also be a symptom.
DIARRHOEA :- dehydration may cause symptom of corona which cause diarrhea.
HEADACHE :- patient may observe headache .
LOSS OF TASTE OR SMELL :- lost of taste and smell is also a big symptom to understand that they body infected with virus.

SERIOUS SYMPTOMS:

DIFFICULTY BREATHING OR SHORTNESS OF BREATH :- it is one of the biggest symptom of corona when lungs got infected and when patient is in critical condition then such symptoms appears so it need medical assistance immediately.

CHEST PAIN OR PRESSURE:- some time patient can feel pressure over chest and pain in his / her back it is also serious symptoms.

LOSS OF SPEECH OR MOVEMENT:- if patient lost speech and unable to move this one is also a serious symptom.

3. DRINK 2 GLASS LUKE WARM WATER EARLY IN THE MORNING . WITH TWO TEA SPOON PURE/NATURAL HONEY. :-

It is good habit to tune your body with some healthy habits which is always good and as equal effective as medicine.

Drinking luke warm water is one of that habit it intoxicated your body and control your weight and increase your immunity level.

during covid situation a patient have to drink warm water through out the day and until the recovery of body from such situation.

if you drink luke warm water with pure honey and lemon then it increase effect on body to maintain its proctection system against any kind of virus and bacteria.

- **4. DRINK HOT MILK WITH SMALL PINCH OF TURMARIC AT NIGHT BEFOR A SLEEP.**

It is always good to have milk with turmeric as turmeric having anti viral ,anti septic qualities.

Turmeric is good to boost energy stamina in body and good for white blood cells.

 so we have to take hot milk with turmeric even milk itself is complete food.

But its quality enhances when a pinch of turmeric added in it.

5. WHAT TO EAT DURING INFECTION BEFORE AND AFTER

•   We have to eat such food which help us to fight against infection .

•   Its only happen when we eat healthy & good food .

•   so we have to eat food full of protein and dietary fiber we have to drink two liter water ,cow milk and butter milk . keep our body hydrated.

•   we have to increase protein intake and eat Almonds Egg ,Paneer ,Pumpkin seeds, Sprouts, Chicken,Millets [ots] ,Milk, broccoli,Peanuts all these are good source of fiber.

6. HOW TO PREPARE HERBAL JUICE AND KADHA.

Herbal juice can be prepare with the following content use two inch stem of Allovera, two three small leaves of zinseng / ashwagandha . use mixer grinder and two or three cup of water and grind well and now steer and drink the juice .

*

* giloy and tulsi this herbs can smash well and now keep on burning gas stove and pour one glass or 250 ML water and after boiling when it remains only half of concentration then separate with help of sieve and drink the juice . it will enhance and boost your immune system.

* Herbal kadha in which you can use along with your two cup of black or green tea use black pepper 5-6 ,one clove, small piece of ginger, dalchini (cinnamon) boil three cup filter the boiled kadha when remain two cup for little taste you can add one tea spoon of honey.

- **7. WHAT TO DO WHEN SOAR THROAT AND THROAT CHOAK.**

You use pain relief and use gargle with common salt or with betadine and cipladine with prescription of doctor .

 use some humidifier and honey and black pepper with sugar or jaggery , or use mulhati a herb use for throat problem.

- **8. WHAT IS BEST HOME REMEDY TO BOOST IMMUNE SYSTEM.**

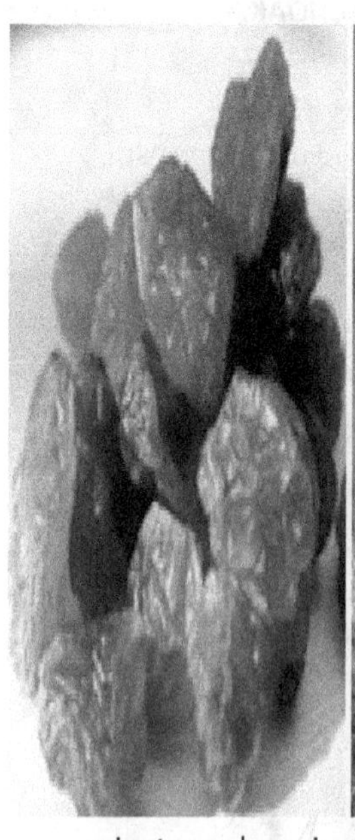

I am telling you about best home remedy which enhance the immunity as well increase your appetite and anti viral and bacterial .

First all we have to take 10-15 raisin munkka big with seeds , remove the seeds of raisin and take half tea spoon of black pepper powder and two pinch of black or common salt . then smash raisin with salt and pepper powder . after mixing well use mixture ball   with fork and then roasted in burning flame.

Roast for two minutes in mild flames and after roasting keep it for cooling use it at moderate temperature .

put in your mouth and chew for five minutes or keep in your mouth and allow mouth to slow down the juice through throat and it works with first and second dose . it is better to take after dinner or after night meal.

- 9. **EFFECTS OF STEAM INHALATION .**

In case of choke of nostrils and throat.

it really relax your throat muscle and increase blood circulation and remove choking elements and clear the path of nostril .

use can use steam of normal water or you can use that steam with carom seeds and eucalyptus leaves .

you can use amirtdhara made up of bhimsaini kapoor, satpudina, loha bhashm . clove oil .nilgiri oil and sat of ajwain.

- **10. USE GREEN TEA AND KEEP HYDRATED YOUR BODY .**

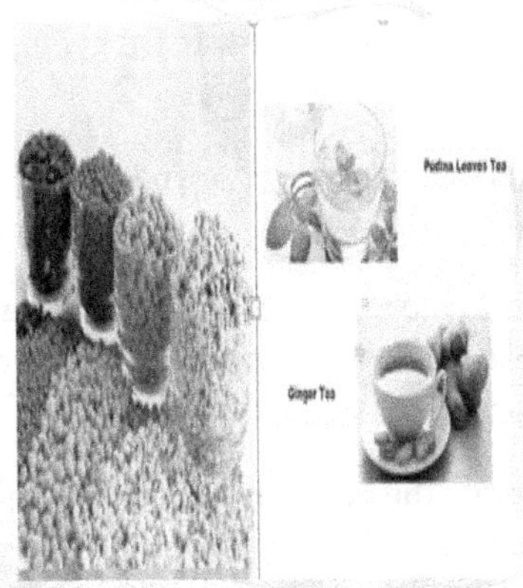

Green tea have vital effect on our body it having anti oxidant elements.

It help in good health of lungs it increase stamina of lungs and reduce weight and strengthen the immune system.

-
-

- **11 EAT MILLETS AND PROTEIN BASED DIET.**

- Course grain or millets full fibre , calcium and protein it help to build muscles .which is highly desirable during this pandemic. .

- It clear your motion and increase the health of stomach and digestive system and also good for large and small intestine .

- Its full of vitamin c and vitamin c helps our white blood cells and make our protective .

- It is also found good to maintain health of bones which start decaying at the age of 35 and more.

- **12.EAT APPLE CITRUS FRUITS AND SEASONAL FRUITS.**

Apples is full of antioxidants and vitamin b complex and minerals which help the body to fight with virus and bacteria .

- Citrus fruits like oranges figs , grapes and lemon , sweet lemon etc

- Even banana , mango and any seasonal fruits help to increase oxygen level and antioxidant helps body to protect from virus and bacteria

It not only hydrate the body but also contain fiber which play vital role play in digestion and keeping good health of body.

- **13. DO PHYSICAL ACTIVITIES 15-20 MINUTES.**

it should be in our daily routine to some physical activities.

*	You can do any kind of physical activities like running , walking ,exercising ,cycling and aerobics helps to increase oxygen level of the body.

*	Exercise for 15-20 minutes daily enhance lungs stamina to inhale and exhale . And even all other parts of body Oxygenated due to exercise.

14. DEEP BREATHING AND YOGA MEDITATION.

MEDITATION IN POSTURE OF PADMASHANA

*	You do meditation if you feel to relax your mind . but for good effect of meditation and yoga you should practice under trained teacher.

VAKAASANA

It should be done under able guidance

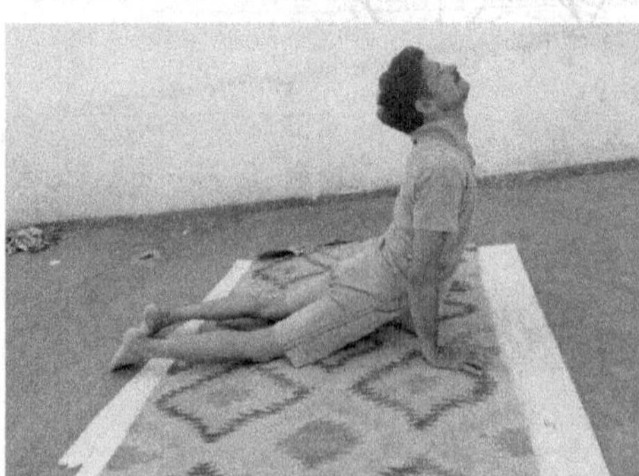

BHUJANG ASANA

Stretch your body posture like snake.

NAUKA ASANA

Stretch your legs and hands in shape of ship (Naav) it reduce belly fats and increase your strength and stamina.

SHIRSHA ASANA

It increase blood circulation in mind at initially you can do with support of side walls otherwise suggested do such yoga under able guidance.

HALASANA

Slowly stretch the body and bend backward like a plough.

TRIKONASANA

Stretch body in both side once with right and left leg and vice -versa.

CHAKRA ASANA

Stretching body like circle it should be tried and able guide.

Yoga asana create flexibility endurance it helps to excretion of dead cells and toxic material from body and increase oxygen level of human body its secretion good hormones' which creates good mood , peace and happiness.

- Meditation helps to concentrate mind to recollect energy and will power of the body it stimulate our immune system.

- **15. KEEP YOUR SELF AWAY FROM NEGATIVE NEWS.**

- always look for positive news because it creates a positive attitude towards the things surround us.

- it enhance the will and energy of body , mind and increase the efficiency of soul and body parts to fight with external enemies so always engage your self in creative and entertaining activities it enhance the will power

- ## 16.ENTERTAIN YOURSELF WITH MUSIC AND COMEDY SHOW.

instead of sitting ideally and waiting for time to normalize the situation we have to read good or interesting story books and good literature .

we have to enjoy every moment gifted by god.

 it will enhance your will power and give more strength and stamina to fight with all kind of disease .

as you heard "man ke haare har man ke jite jeet" it means if we willing to survive than this small virus can not defeat you at any cost .

 if you lay down than virus itself created by the body .

 its totally game of panic and how ease you face the situation.

There is lot of example that many people even at the age of 95 and above even I read about a couple at the age of 105 year and 95. Defeat the corona .

if at this age some body defeat the corona then why can not?

So always stay positive and enjoys with all amenities you have.

- **17. USE SANITIZER , HAND WASH , WEAR A MASK.**

- this reduce your risk to get infected

- so always wear a mask

- until condition not changed i means to say until   vaccination done

- or we get heard immunity

- we should continue with available safety methods to protect our lives.

- **18.KEEP YOUR SELF AWAY FROM SOCIAL GATHERING.**

- AVOID WEDDING FUNCTIONS:- daily routine life it is good to enjoy the wedding and other functions because they are great source of entertainment . but they also great source of gathering so we should avoid the gathering because it increase our chance to get infected.

RALLYS :- may be there is political issue which you find more important . but nothing more important then your life so you should avoid such gathering any protest , rally and election gathering.

• PUBLIC PLACES:- we have to avoid parks , bus stand , railway station and all other kind of public places if not required then do not visit hospitals too because it increase our probability to get infected.

• MARKETS :- Do not even visit to market places until it is not required at all if you visiting for any reason then try to collect all required materials so you need to visit market places frequently.

PUBLIC PARKS , MALLS AND CINEMA HALLS:- as malls and cinema halls are big source of mass gathering to avoid such gathering don't visit such places.it increase your probablity to get infected

19. GET VACCINATED AT YOUR EARLIEST :- as soon as you vaccinated it will protect you from infection as a medicine it works as well as you feel confident that such infection can not harm you as you vaccinated so that positive mind set help to develop Confidence and inner strength against covid-19.

thanks for purchase and reading this book its great matter of pleasure that my knowledge or information shared with you help you little bit ......with love

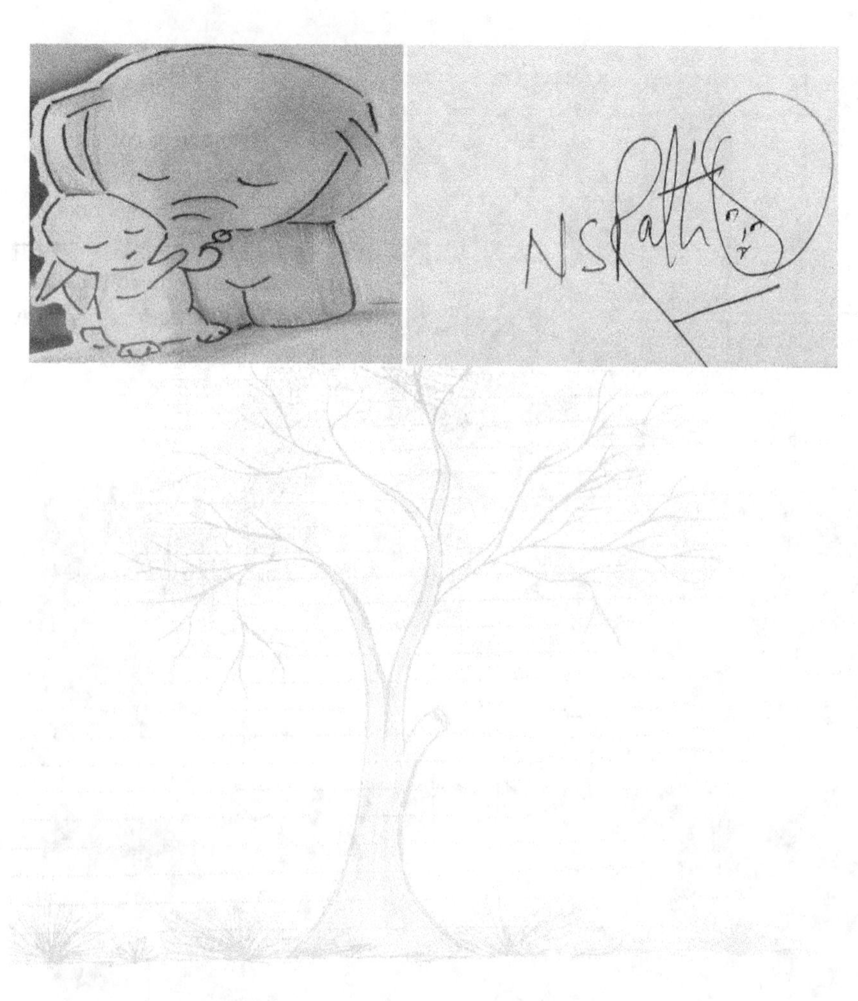